NOTE TO PARENTS

Welcome to Kingfisher Readers! This program is designed to help young readers build skills, confidence, and a love of reading as they explore their favorite topics.

These tips can help you get more from the experience of reading books together. But remember, the most important thing is to make reading fun!

Tips to Warm Up Before Reading

- Ask your child to share what they already know about the topic.
- Preview the pages, pictures, sub-heads and captions, so your reader will have an idea what is coming.
- Share your questions. What are you both wondering about?

While Reading

- Stop and think at the end of each section. What was that about?
- Let the words make pictures in your minds. Share what you see.
- When you see a new word, talk it over. What does it mean?
- Do you have more questions? Wonder out loud!

After Reading

- Share the parts that were most interesting or surprising.
- Make connections to other books, similar topics, or experiences.
- Discuss what you'd like to know more about. Then find out!

With five distinct levels and a wealth of appealing topics, the Kingfisher Readers series provides children with an exciting way to learn to read about the world around them. Enjoy!

Ellie Costa, M.S. Ed.
Literacy Specialist, Bank Street School for Children, New York

KINGFISHER READERS

level **4**

Human Body

Anita Ganeri

KINGFISHER
NEW YORK

KINGFISHER
LONDON & NEW YORK

Distributed in the U.S. and Canada by Macmillan,
175 Fifth Ave., New York, NY 10010

Library of Congress Cataloging-in-Publication data has been applied for.

Series editor: Thea Feldman
Literacy consultant: Ellie Costa, Bank Street College, New York
Text for U.S. edition written by Thea Feldman

ISBN: 978-0-7534-6962-0 (HB)
ISBN: 978-0-7534-6931-6 (PB)

Kingfisher books are available for special promotions
and premiums. For details contact: Special Markets Department,
Macmillan, 175 Fifth Ave., New York, NY 10010.

For more information, please visit
www.kingfisherbooks.com

Printed in China
9 8 7 6 5 4 3 2 1
1TR/1012/WKT/UG/105MA

Picture credits
The Publisher would like to thank the following for permission to reproduce their material. Every care
has been taken to trace copyright holders. However, if there have been unintentional omissions or failure
to trace copyright holders, we apologize and will, if informed, endeavor to make corrections in any future
edition.
(t = top; b = bottom; c = center; l = left; r = right):
Cover Corbis/Tim Clayton; Pages 3t Shutterstock/Ralf Juergen Kraft; 3ct Shutterstock/Monkey
Business Images; 3c KF Archive; 3cb Shutterstock/doglikehorse; 3b Corbis/John W. Karapelou,
CMI; 4l KF Archive; 4-5 Shutterstock/Mandy Godbehear; 5t KF Archive; 6t Shutterstock/xpixel; 6b
Shutterstock/Williv; 7 Shutterstock/Ralf Juergen Kraft; 8l KF Archive; 8r KF Archive; 9t KF Archive;
9bl Shutterstock/DenisNata; 9bc Shutterstock/doglikehorse; 9br Shutterstock/Palmer Kane LLC;
10 KF Archive; 11t Corbis/Creasource; 11b KF Archive; 12 Corbis/John W. Karapelou, CMI; 13 KF
Archive; 14 KF Archive; 15t KF Archive; 15b KF Archive; 16l Alamy/arlyons; 16r KF Archive; 17t
KF Archive; 17b Shutterstock/Xidong Luo; 18 KF Archive; 19 Corbis/Tim Clayton; 20 KF Archive;
21t KF Archive; 21b Corbis/Laura Doss; 22t Corbis/Creasource; 22b KF Archive; 23 KF Archive; 24
KF Archive; 25t KF Archive; 25b Alamy/ableimages; 26t KF Archive; 26b Corbis/Kevin RL Hanson;
27tr Shutterstock/Rob Marmion; 27b Corbis/Randy Faris; 28 Corbis/Janie Airey/Cutural; 29t
Shutterstock/ Monkey Business Images; 29b Corbis/Marnie Burkhart; 31 Corbis/Tim Clayton

Contents

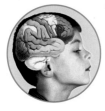

Your body

Your body works for you all the time. Here are some things it does while you read this book. Your eyes see the words. Your brain tells you what they mean. Muscles in your hands hold the book. Your heart pumps blood. And your lungs take in air so you can breathe.

Heart

Lungs

Bone

Cells

Your body is made up of millions and millions of tiny **cells**. Most cells are so small you need to use a **microscope** to see them. Cells work together to do many jobs for your body. Two common types of cells are red and white blood cells.

Red blood cells

White blood cells

The human body is amazing. It has so many parts that work together without you being aware of them. And every person has the same basic body parts. Let's explore some of the ways the human body works.

Skeleton

A skeleton is made up of 206 bones. Bones are very hard and strong and they keep your body together. The largest is the thighbone. The smallest is in your ear. Some bones protect your **internal organs**. Your skull bones, for example, protect your brain. Your rib bones protect your heart and lungs.

Strong but still breakable

The X-ray photograph shows a broken bone. A broken bone can grow back together. Sometimes a cast is needed to keep the bone in place so it heals properly.

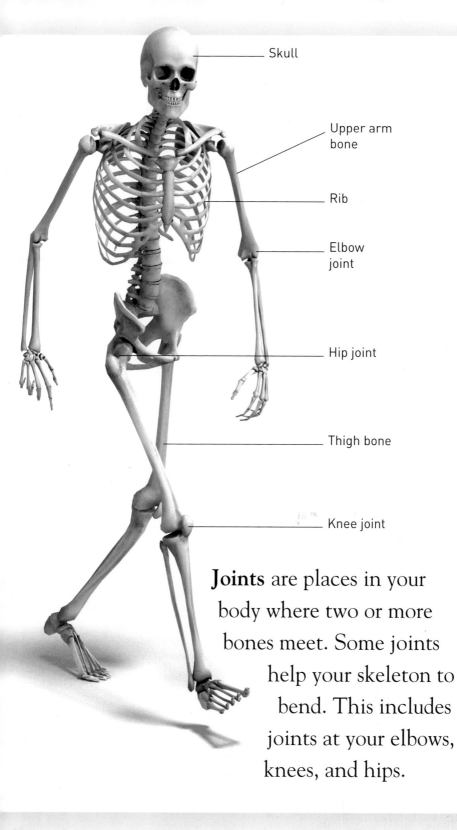

Skull

Upper arm
bone

Rib

Elbow
joint

Hip joint

Thigh bone

Knee joint

Joints are places in your
body where two or more
bones meet. Some joints
help your skeleton to
bend. This includes
joints at your elbows,
knees, and hips.

Muscles

Your bones do not move by themselves. They need muscles to help them. You have about 640 muscles in your body. Many of them are attached to your bones by **tendons**. Tendons are strong bands that work with your bones and muscles to get you moving!

Your muscles come in many different sizes. Together, they make up about one third of your body weight.

You use a lot of muscles when you play sports.

You have muscles from head to toe.

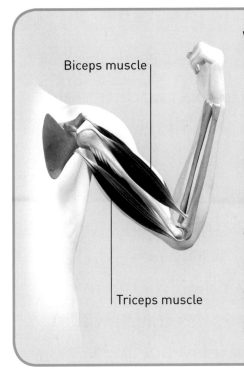

Biceps muscle

Triceps muscle

Working in pairs

Some muscles work in pairs. This includes the triceps and biceps in your upper arms. The biceps pulls to bend your arm, and the triceps relaxes. The triceps pulls to straighten your arm, and the biceps relaxes.

Some muscles do not move your bones. They do other jobs. Muscles make your heart beat. Other muscles help you **digest** your food. Tiny muscles in your face move so you can smile, blink, and make funny faces.

Skin and hair

Your body is covered in layers of skin. Skin protects your body from **germs** and dirt. It also helps your body stay at the right temperature.

The top layer is called the epidermis. The epidermis is waterproof. The next layer is called the dermis. This is where new skin cells are made. They push their way up to the surface. Your body is always making new skin cells. Below the dermis is a layer of fat.

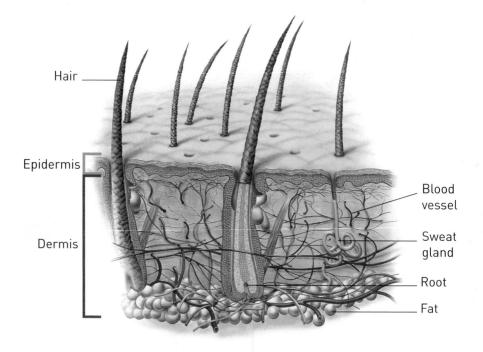

Hair

Epidermis

Dermis

Blood vessel

Sweat gland

Root

Fat

Hair grows from the dermis layer of your skin. You, like other **mammals**, have hair growing over most of your body. Hair helps protect your body. It keeps you warm too.

Sweat glands are also in the dermis. When you get too hot, the glands release a liquid called sweat. The sweat goes up to the epidermis and helps you cool down.

Fingerprints

Fingerprints are tiny patterns in the skin on your fingertips. They help you grip things. No two people have the same fingerprints.

Brain and nerves

The brain of an adult person weighs about 3 pounds (1.4 kilograms). That may seem small, but the brain does a huge job. It helps you make sense of everything around you. And it controls how you learn, what you think, and how you feel.

The brain has many parts. Each part controls something else in your body, everything from breathing and blinking to reacting to what is happening near you.

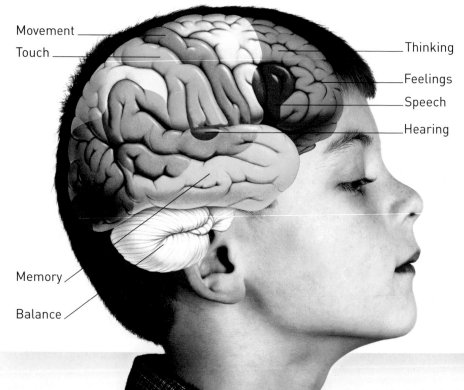

Movement

Touch

Thinking

Feelings

Speech

Hearing

Memory

Balance

Nerves

Spinal cord

The brain is connected to the rest of your body by the spinal cord. The spinal cord is made up of nerves that run like long, thin wires, from the brain to the rest of the body. The spinal cord is protected by the body's bony spine.

Messages travel through the nerves between the brain and other body parts. For example, if your hand is close to a flame, your brain will tell it to move.

Funny bone

Have you ever banged your elbow and felt a weird or funny tingling? You've hit your "funny bone"! But it's not a bone at all. It's really a large nerve that lies close to the surface of your skin. When you hit your elbow the nerve bumps against a bone in your arm.

Sight and hearing

You have five senses, including sight and hearing. You see with your eyes and hear with your ears.

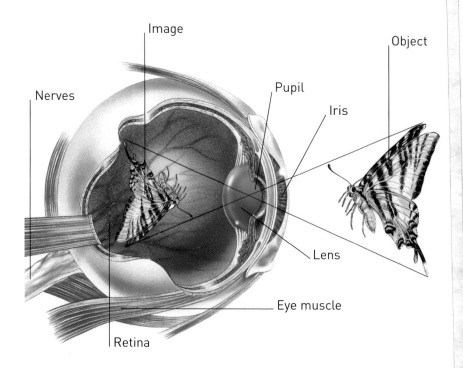

Image

Object

Pupil

Nerves

Iris

Lens

Eye muscle

Retina

You see things when light bounces off objects and goes into each eye through the **pupil**. The lens focuses the light on the **retina** at the back of your eye, where it makes an upside-down picture of what you are seeing. Nerves send this picture to your brain. Your brain knows to turn the picture right side up.

Sound travels deep inside your ears.

You hear things when sound travels inside your ear and down a long tube called the ear canal. The sound hits a piece of thin skin called the eardrum. The eardrum shakes or vibrates. Tiny bones pick up the vibrations and send them deeper inside the ear, where there is liquid. The liquid vibrates too and pulls on nerves that send messages to the brain.

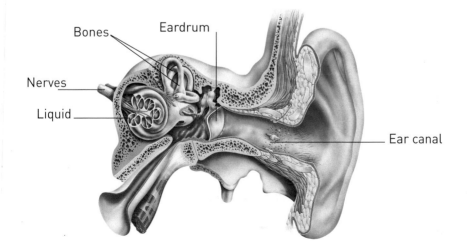

Bones

Eardrum

Nerves

Liquid

Ear canal

Taste, smell, and touch

Your other three senses are taste, smell, and touch. You taste with your tongue, smell with your nose, and touch with your skin.

Your tongue is covered with thousands of tiny bumps called taste buds. The taste buds pick up the flavors of food. Nerves send messages about the flavors to your brain.

Taste buds

Your tongue can taste sweet things, like ice cream. It can taste salty, sour, and bitter things too.

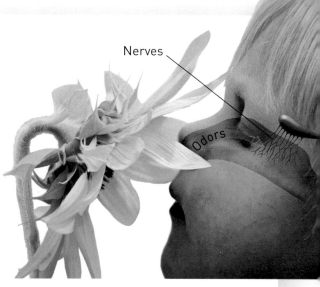

Nerves

Odors

When you breathe in, air and odors enter the openings in your nose. Nerves inside your nose send messages about the odors to your brain.

Your skin has millions of tiny nerves that help you touch and feel things. The nerves tell your brain whether things are hot, cold, hard, soft, or something else.

Most sensitive

Your most sensitive skin is on your fingertips, lips, and toes. They have the most nerve cells. That means they sense the slightest touch easily.

Lungs

To stay alive, the human body needs oxygen.
Oxygen is a gas you can't see but it is in the
air you breathe through your nose or mouth.
With every breath you take, air goes down
your **windpipe** and into your lungs. There,
the oxygen passes into your blood. Your blood
carries oxygen to all the parts of your body.

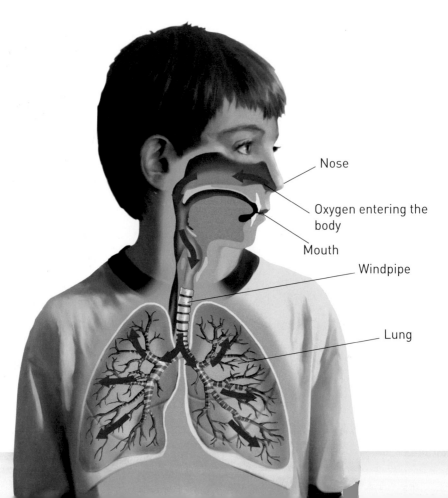

Nose

Oxygen entering the body

Mouth

Windpipe

Lung

As your body uses oxygen, it makes a gas called carbon dioxide, which it doesn't need. The gas passes from your blood to your lungs. It is removed from your body when you breathe out.

You breathe harder when you exercise to send more oxygen to your muscles.

Breathing

When you breathe in, your chest muscles lift your ribs up and out so that your chest gets bigger and your lungs have space to fill up with fresh air. When you breathe out, your ribs move in and down. This squeezes used air out of your lungs and out through your nose or mouth.

Heart and blood

Put your hand over the left side of your chest. You can feel your heart beating! Your heart is a very special muscle about the size of your clenched fist. With each beat your heart pumps blood through your body. It beats between 80 and 100 times a minute.

This is what happens every time your heart beats.

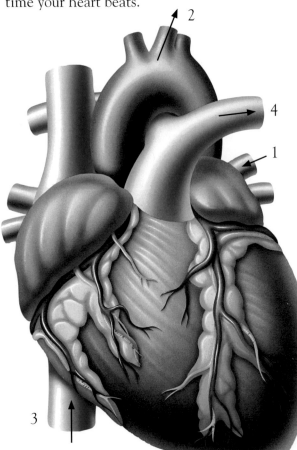

1. Oxygen-rich blood from your lungs flows into your heart.

2. Your heart pumps the blood to the rest of your body.

3. Blood needing oxygen flows from your body into your heart.

4. The blood is pumped to your lungs to pick up more oxygen.

Blood flows around your body in tiny tubelike **blood vessels**. Blood vessels called arteries carry oxygen-rich blood. Vessels called veins carry blood that needs more oxygen.

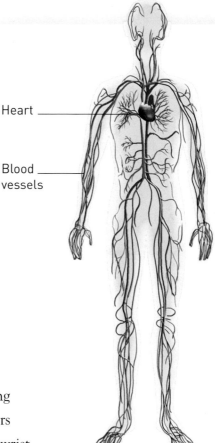

Heart

Blood vessels

A doctor can feel the blood pumping through your body by pressing fingers lightly on the blood vessels in your wrist.

Digestion

There are things in food called **nutrients** that your body needs to stay healthy. To get the nutrients, your body first has to break down food and change it. This is called digestion. Digestion starts when your teeth bite into food.

Two sets of teeth

You are born without teeth. By the time you are three, you have 20 "baby teeth." When you are around six, those teeth start to fall out and are replaced by 32 "adult teeth."

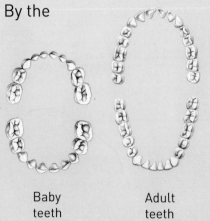

Baby teeth

Adult teeth

1. Your teeth chew food. Saliva, a liquid in your mouth, makes the food slippery and easy to swallow.

2. The food travels to the stomach down a long tube called the esophagus.

3. In the stomach, food mixes with digestive juices. It becomes thick and souplike. Then it moves to the small intestine.

4. In the small intestine, more juices mix with the food. The useful parts of the food pass through the thin walls of the small intestine into your blood and are carried to other parts of your body.

5. The parts of food your body can't use go into the large intestine. You pass them out of your body as waste.

Liver and kidneys

After blood picks up food from the small intestine it passes through the liver. The liver removes any toxins or poisons to make the food safe. It also takes some of the nutrients and stores them until your body needs them.

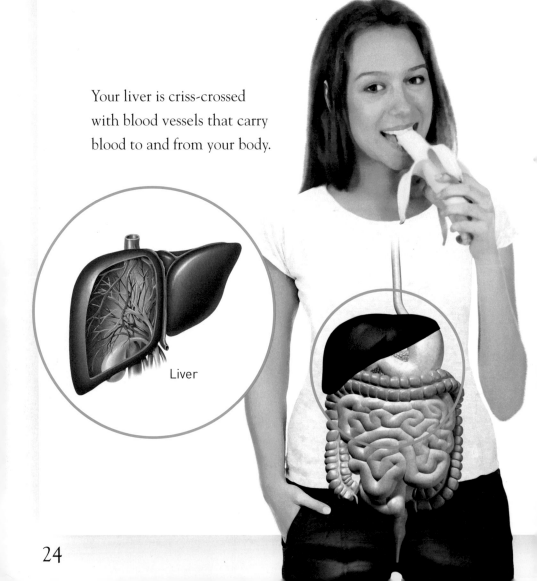

Your liver is criss-crossed with blood vessels that carry blood to and from your body.

Liver

Kidneys

Bladder

You have two, bean-shaped kidneys in your lower back. They clean your blood and take out waste that could harm your body. They also get rid of any extra water that your body does not need.

The waste and extra water become a liquid called **urine**. Urine flows down two tubes from the kidneys to the **bladder**. The bladder stores urine until you feel the need to empty it.

Drink up!
A healthy bladder can comfortably hold two 8-ounce (0.25-liter) glasses of liquid for up to five hours.

25

Birth and growth

The human body is amazing. And that includes the very beginning of life. Everybody starts life inside their mother's **womb**. After growing for about nine months a baby is born!

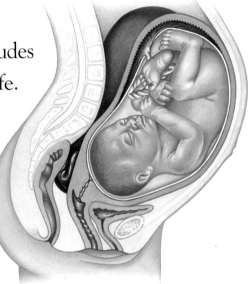

A baby cannot do very much without help. Babies cannot walk or talk for months. But they grow and learn quickly for the first two years. Then babies become toddlers. They can do many more things on their own.

A baby turns upside-down when he or she is ready to be born.

A baby crawls, then learns to walk.

A period of fast growth is often called a "growth spurt." Most people have a growth spurt for the first two years of their lives. Then they have a second one around age ten. The human body stops growing around age 20, but it never stops changing.

In sickness and health

When you were very young you probably had **vaccinations**. Vaccinations protect you from getting some illnesses. Many illnesses happen because germs get inside the body. When you catch a cold, for example, it's because germs called **viruses** have gotten inside your body.

Your body often fights off illnesses on its own. Sometimes, though, you need to see the doctor and get some medicine. Medicine can help you feel better.

This nurse is giving a child a vaccination.

Staying healthy

There is a lot you can do to stay healthy. You can eat a lot of fresh fruits and vegetables. And you can exercise for about an hour every day. It's also important to get a lot of sleep and to keep your body clean. These things will make it easier for your body to fight off germs and diseases.

Glossary

bladder the part of the body that collects and holds urine

blood vessels tubes that carry blood all over your body

cells the tiny units that make up every part of your body

digest to break down food into nutrients and waste

germs tiny living things that can cause illnesses

internal organs parts inside the body, such as the brain and heart, that do important jobs

joints places where two or more bones meet

mammals animals that have hair or fur on their bodies and that make milk to give their young

microscope a machine that lets you see very tiny things up close

nerves cells like long, thin wires that carry messages between your body and brain

nutrients parts of food that are good for the body

pupil the opening in the center of the eye through which light enters

retina the area at the back of your eye that has lots of sensitive nerve cells

tendons strong bands that attach your muscles to your bones

urine a waste liquid made by your body

vaccinations shots that protect you from some types of illnesses

viruses tiny living things that cause some illnesses and diseases

windpipe a tube that carries air into and out of your lungs; also called the trachea

womb the part of a mother's body in which babies grow until they are born

Index

If you have enjoyed reading
this book, look out for more in
the Kingfisher Readers series!

**Collect
and read
them all!**

KINGFISHER READERS: LEVEL 4

Flight ☐
Human Body ☐
Pirates ☐
Sharks ☐
Weather ☐

KINGFISHER READERS: LEVEL 5

Ancient Egyptians ☐
Hurricanes ☐
Space ☐
Rainforests ☐
Record Breakers—The Fastest ☐

For a full list of Kingfisher Readers books, plus
guidance for teachers and parents and activities
and fun stuff for kids, go to the Kingfisher Readers
website: www.kingfisherreaders.com